Quimper Pottery

Ann Marie O'Neill

POTIERS BRETONS

Schiffer
Publishing Ltd

77 Lower Valley Road, Atglen, PA 19310

QUIMPER FAIENCES

Title page: Large figural piece of Breton potters called *"Potiers Bretons."* Photo courtesy of Musée de la Faïence Jules Verlingue

ISBN: 0-88740-650-5

Copyright © 1994 by Ann Marie O'Neill
Library of Congress Catalog Number: 94--65615

Printed in Hong Kong
We are interested in hearing from authors with book ideas on related topics.

Published by Schiffer Publishing Ltd.
77 Lower Valley Road
Atglen, PA 19310
Please write for a free catalog.
This book may be purchased from the publisher.
Please include $2.95 postage.
Try your bookstore first.

CONTENTS

Dedicated to my husband and friend, Fred, whose patience, love and support helped to make this book possible.

Workers in the faïencerie, c. 1920.

ACKNOWLEDGMENTS

Many people have contributed in many ways, both great and small, to the realization of this book. I extend my deepest gratitude to all, but most especially to my daughter Beth O'Neill Maloney for her enthusiastic editorial support and to my son Bill for his technical support. I was computer illiterate when I began this project so Bill faced a daunting task!

My heartfelt thanks to Millicent Mali, who graciously enriched my knowledge and love of French faience over the years.

FRANCE

Chapter 1

HISTORY: the town of Quimper and start of pottery production

Quimper, a small city in the French province of Brittany, 350 miles east of Paris, is set alongside the Odet River, tucked neatly into a notch surrounded by verdant hills. The Cathedral of St. Corentin, whose spires can be seen from almost everywhere in Quimper, is the dominant feature of the town. The faïence of Quimper can also be seen almost everywhere - in shop windows, museums, the tourist office, restaurants and adorning the doors of the faïencerie. In fact, the faïence of Quimper has become synonymous with the town and is collected and treasured in many countries of the world.

Just how does one pronounce "Quimper" and what exactly is "faïence"? Faïence is simply the French word for tin glazed pottery and a faïencerie is a factory where pottery is produced. To unravel the mystery surrounding the pronunciation of Quimper we must go back to the fifth century when the Celts settled in Brittany, establishing a village at the confluence or juncture of the Steir and Odet Rivers. Because the Celtic word for such a juncture is *kemper* the village

came to be known as Kemper. Some time later, the spelling was changed from "Kemper" to "Quimper", but the pronunciation remained the same, *kem-pair'*. As you approach the town on any of today's main thoroughfares, you are greeted by a sign reading:

Quimper's welcoming signs are posted in French and in the original Breton. **Remember the Breton spelling when pronouncing Quimper.**

Quimper is a modern city of 60,000. Construction of the gothic Cathedral of Saint Corentin was begun in 1239 and was not completed until 1494, some 250 years later. Extensive renovations are currently in progress. The spires of the Cathedral tower over the Odet River.

Pardon scene by Jim Sevellec

Today the people of Brittany, many of whom are descendants of these early Celts, treasure their heritage. The proud Bretons continue to use the Breton language, a form of Gaelic, and observe many Celtic customs and traditions. The spirit of Breton culture is reflected in the faïence of Quimper and surely accounts for its great popularity. Indeed, the Breton countryside, with its rolling green hills, light morning mists, grazing animals and small fishing villages could easily be mistaken for Scotland or Wales.

Music and dance, so often illustrated on the wares of Quimper, have always been a part of Breton celebrations, be they weddings, religious festivals called *pardons* or the annual Festival of Cornouaille in July, a week long festival of art, music, dance, theatre, Breton games, food and more. Even today, on festival days many Bretons dress in their ancestral costumes, the men in their colorful, puffy pants called *bragoubraz* and the ladies in their high, starched *coiffes* or headdresses. To a collector of the faïence of Quimper it seems as though these beautifully clad Bretons just emerged from a favorite plate.

Pottery making began in Brittany in Gallo-Roman times and was an active industry in the Middle Ages. All of the natural resources needed for a faïencerie were in abundant supply in the region: clay along the riverbanks; wood from the vast forests to fuel the drying ovens; and of course, the river for transporting the finished product.

Modern pottery production began in 1690 when Jean Baptiste Bousquet, a potter of some distinction in the south of France, established a faïencerie in Quimper on the banks of the Odet River. For almost one hundred years Bousquet's faïencerie had a monopoly on the pottery business in Quimper. But, as often happens, a Grande Maison employee, François Eloury, broke away and established Quimper's second faïencerie, later known as the Porquier factory. In 1778, Guillaume Dumaine founded the third faïencerie in Quimper. Dumaine's faïencerie, which produced primarily *grès* or stoneware, later became known as the Henriot factory.

The Quimper faïencerie in 1993.

The door handles of the faïencerie are made of tiles bearing traditional Breton figures, rendered in exquisite detail and flanked by sprays of *ajonc* on the left and *breuyere* on the right, bordered by a vivid blue on blue *décor riche* border.

A closer look!

The Rouen décor was introduced in the eighteenth century by Pierre Caussy, who came to Quimper from a family of faïence artists in Rouen. This is a later example of Caussy's Rouen décor and was produced by the Porquier faïencerie. Triangular shaped wall pocket bearing the coat of arms of Brittany. 16" long, 8 1/2" wide, 4 1/2" deep, PB

These plates, bearing naive yet detailed figures, were produced c.1880-90 by the Grande Maison. The figures are carefully drawn and their poses are amusing. 8 1/4" diameter, HB, c.1890.

Chapter Two

THE QUIMPER POTTERY FACTORIES

- Jean Baptiste Bousquet, 1690
Grande Maison factory

The early wares produced by Jean Baptiste Bousquet's faïencerie were the common tablewares used in most Breton homes. These wares are very difficult to identify because they were usually undecorated and unsigned. Very few have survived.

Bousquet's faïencerie, later known as the Grande Maison because of its imposing size and location on the *rue Haute* or high road, was directed by succeeding generations, including Bousquet's son-in-law, Pierre Clement Caussy. Caussy, a third generation potter from Rouen, directed the factory during its golden age, the eighteenth century, producing exquisite wares inspired by the pottery of Rouen and Nevers. The business flourished. Additional drying ovens were constructed. *Grès*, a heavy stoneware, was introduced and Caussy employed more than one hundred workers.

Antoine de la Hubaudière, Caussy's son-in-law, succeeded him and the de la Hubaudière family continued to direct the faïencerie until 1915.

In 1882, the Grande Maison registered their first mark, "HB", representing the de la Hubaudière (H) name and the founders name, Bousquet (B). The Grande Maison's second mark, slightly different than the first mark, was registered in 1883. In 1904 the word "Quimper" was added to the "HB" mark to distinguish wares made in Quimper from the imitations being produced elsewhere in France. This "HB Quimper" mark was used from 1904 until 1983, making it difficult to date wares bearing this mark. From 1968 to 1983 some wares were stamped with the half circle mark.

Rare plaque in relief featuring a handsome Breton with his walking stick. Stylized flowers alternate with pierced shapes on the border. Marked with the first HB mark that is so rare! 11" long, 7" wide. 1870.

This *Petit Breton* pattern produced by the Grande Maison HB has a naive charm. It is a classic, sometimes done in blue and red. 8 1/4" diameter, HBQ, c.1935.

A primitive Breton carrying his walking stick with birds overhead and a simple *a la touche* border combine to give this plate its country charm. 7 1/2" diameter, HBQ, c.1910.

A charming, little tea pot with cut corner panels in a tennis pattern . A demure Bretonne in the center . 6" tall, 5 1/2" across, HBQ, c.1935.

This Breton gentleman stands between two *arbustes* or shrubs of red and blue. The border is an alternating pattern of blue and red *touches*. HBQ, 9" diameter, c.1920.

The Grande Maison produced a tremendous variety of wares in a myriad of shapes and patterns, including an art deco line signed "Odetta". Some of the shapes and patterns produced in the HB factory were distinctly theirs and some are very similar to those produced in the other faïenceries of Quimper. With experience, you will instinctively recognize many of the wares produced only by the Grande Maison.

A sweet *porte alumettes* (literally, a holder for matches) is marked simply "HB". 3 1/2" long, 19th century. This early mark brings a higher price than a similar piece marked "HB *Quimper*".

Delicately rendered in soft tones, this trefoil serving dish features a dapper gentleman and a lovely lady. HBQ, 10 1/2" x 11", c.1910.

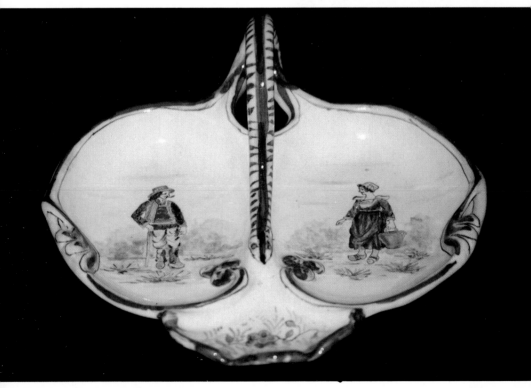

The form of this vase is elegant. A pensive Breton man gazes off into the distance. Blue on blue *décor riche* surrounds the center panel. The pair of lion heads above are fabulous! 17" tall, HBQ, c.1925.

Graceful form and superb décor combine in this magnificent vase. 13" tall, HBQ, c.1925.

A 7 1/4" covered butter dish is bordered in the *décor riche* pattern and features a lovely Bretonne lady with her basket of eggs. HBQ, c.1930.

The Grande Maison's version of the *décor riche* border surrounds a carefully painted Breton couple examining their duck. 9 1/4" diameter, HBQ, c.1935.

Pair of 6" plates in the Rouen décor of 1945. HBQ.

This large double inkstand has wonderful color, exquisite form, and a delightful musician. 11" long, 8 1/2" wide and 2" tall, HBQ, c.1930.

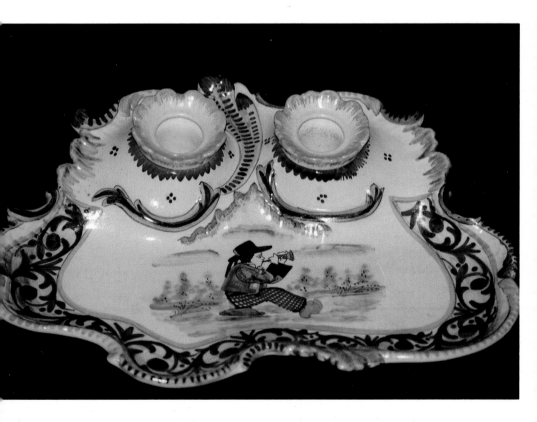

Footed tile in the *Breton Broderie* décor. 5 1/2", HBQ, c.1925.

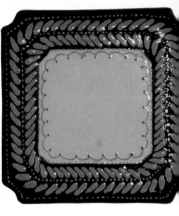

The inspiration for the *Breton Broderie* décor was a popular embroidery pattern often used on Breton costumes. The teapot is 5" tall, the creamer is 2" tall, HB Quimper, c.1925-30.

Breton boderie décor surrounds the figure on this double spouted jug. About 7" long, 5 1/2" tall, HBQ, c.1925.

Very unusual décor on the deco era vase. Deep cobalt blue is banded in gold . The white dots are raised (also called *Breton Broderie*). 5" tall, HBQ, c.1925.

A dramatic example of the *Broderie* décor with *a la poire* décoration. 10" diameter, HBQ, c.1925.

A small but exquisite form with dramatic blue décor. 5" long, HBQ, c.1940.

A boldly decorated 10 1/2" charger with a scalloped rim. Vivid color. HBQ, c.1940.

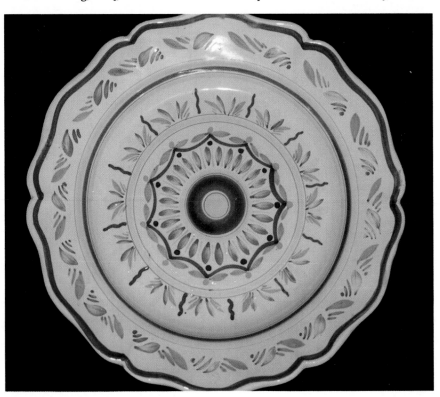

A later edition of "Annaik" from the Grande Maison. 5" tall, HBQ, c.1940.

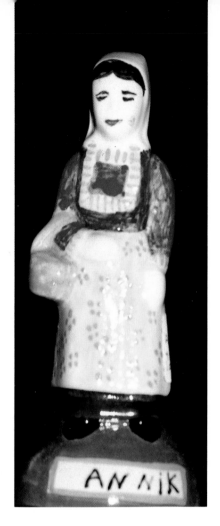

A charming inkwell in the classic Grande Maison *Petit Breton* pattern. 3" tall, 2 1/4" square, HBQ, c.1935.

This c.1940 stoneware pitcher with a Celtic inspired white and blue band is a modern example of the stoneware produced by Quimper's faïenceries in the eighteenth and nineteenth centuries. 4" tall, HBQ.

A 4" tall pitcher decorated with a colorful butterfly! HBQ, c.1930.

Individual *soupière* painted in soft colors. 6 1/2" tall, 6" diameter, HBQ, c.1915-20.

The seated man and the stooped over woman, each with two baskets, are figural double salts in the Art Deco or Art Moderne style of the 1920s and 1930s. He is 3 1/2" tall, 6" long, and 4" wide. She is 5" tall. Both are marked HBQ, c.1935.

An oval vegetable platter with a *sujet ordinaire* and the *couronnes* border pattern. 10" long, 2" tall, HBQ, c.1935.

A dancing Breton couple grace this 6" long and 5" wide scallop shell. Marked *Crepes Gavottes Quimper*, HBQ, c.1935.

Wonderful handled basket decorated entirely in blue, reminiscent of Delftware. The center panel features a basket of flowers with cornucopias on either side. 12" long, 8" tall, HBQ, c.1930.

An eight-piece cider set. The jug features a Breton man clad in pink *bragoubraz* or puffy pants and a pink shirt. He carries a basket, perhaps on his way to market. On each cup there is a bust of a Breton man or woman. HBQ, jug is 9" tall, c.1935.

Six *pots de crème* with tray which features a pipe-smoking Breton flanked by lovely blossoms. Each pot features either a *biniou* playing Breton or a Bretonne with a basket of eggs. Tray is 8" long and 5" wide. HBQ, c.1935

All of the pieces in this tobacco set are exquisitely decorated. The figures are carefully rendered and the backgrounds are wonderful, with soft blended colors. Blue on blue *décor riche* adorns each piece. The tray is 8" in diameter. HBQ, c. 1935.

A striking pair of 4" tall vases, in vivid colors, with beautifully rendered figures. HBQ, c.1935.

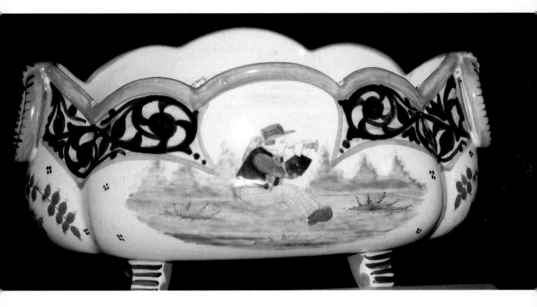

A vividly decorated, footed *jardinière* bears the *décor riche* border, a horn player, and floral sprays. 9" long, 6" wide and 5" tall, HBQ, c.1935.

A pair of 8 1/2" diameter plates. A demure figure graces each plate. HBQ, c.1935.

Two inkwells from the Grande Maison,
c.1940-45. On the left, a 3 1/2" diameter
inkwell in a classic HB décor. On the right,
an inkwell in the same décor. 5" diameter.
Both signed HBQ.

Candlesticks are difficult to find and a
matched pair is a treasure. This 8" tall pair
has four raised panels on each base. HBQ,
c.1935.

Fishing is an important industry in Brittany and the fisherman's life is often reflected in the faïence of Quimper. A *petit* pair of boats for salt! 3 1/2" long, 4" wide, HBQ, c.1935.

A piggy bank for your coins marked with the name "Claude". Tan glaze with pink accents. 8" long, HBQ, c.1945.

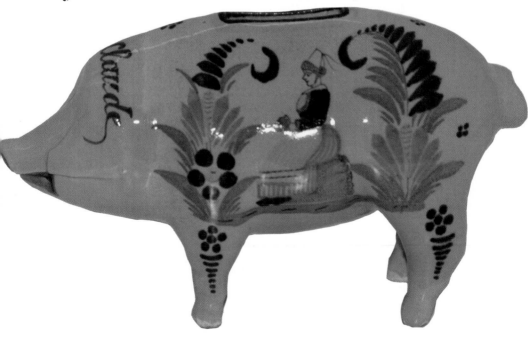

A pair of *Petit Breton* pitchers, 4 1/2" tall,
HBQ, c.1940-45.

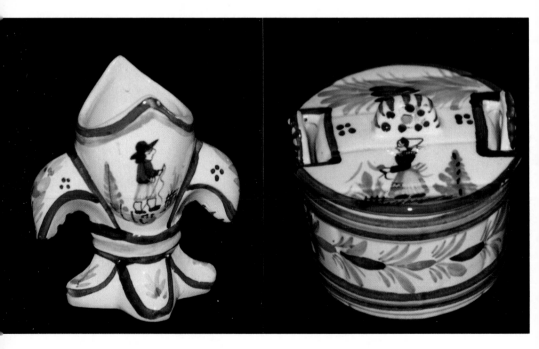

The classic *fleur de lys* form of this *petite porte-bouquet* is sweet! 4" tall, 3 3/4" wide, HBQ, c.1940-45.

An individual jam or butter pot. 2" tall, 2 1/2" diameter, HBQ, c.1945.

An inkwell in the shape of a duck with green sponging on the chest and cobalt blue, green and orange feathers. 5" long, HBQ, c.1935.

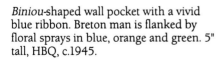

Biniou-shaped wall pocket with a vivid blue ribbon. Breton man is flanked by floral sprays in blue, orange and green. 5" tall, HBQ, c.1945.

Art Deco era bell in a delightful form. The Bretonne lady has a sweet expression. 3 1/2" tall, HBQ, c.1925.

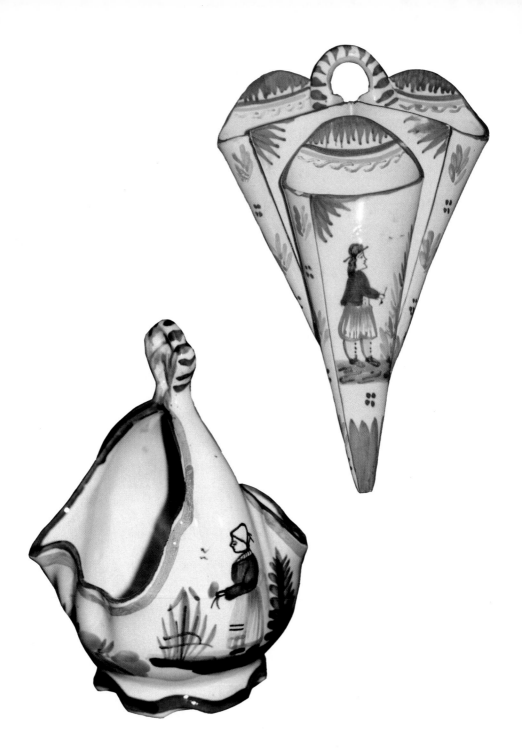

A *cache pot* from the Grande Maison. An appealing form. 5" tall, HBQ, c.1940.

Triple wall pocket for blossoms from your garden. 8" tall, HBQ, c.1940.

The Grande Maison produced this huge *soupière.* 14" including handles, 8" tall, HBQ, c.1940.

This magnificent *jardinière* has a very graceful form and is bordered in vivid yellow and blue. Dainty flowers flank a carefully rendered Bretonne who is probably resting on her way to market to sell her eggs! 5" tall, 14" long, HBQ, c.1930.

Grand coffee pot decorated with *bleuets* and a Bretonne lady. 11" tall, HBQ, c.1945.

A 5" vase for a small bouquet. HBQ, c.1945.

Set of five knife rests, 3" long. Panels are alternately decorated with blue stripes and traditional floral sprays. HBQ, c.1935.

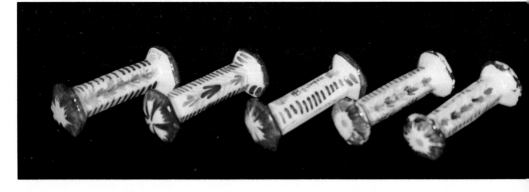

Delicate, soft colors decorate this *biberon* from the Grande Maison. A lovely Bretonne is flanked by lightly drawn blue sprays. The handle and spout are sponged in blue. HBQ, 7" tall, c.1915.

A 7" plate by Lachaud. A simple sketch of the Breton countryside. HBQ, c.1930.

Shield shaped saucer
decorated with one of
Alfred Beau's
Botanique patterns. 5"
x 5 3/4", PB, c.1890.

Jonquils adorn this
lovely 8 1/4" diameter
deeply scalloped bowl
marked simply PB; the
glaze is tinged with
blue; a graceful form.
c.1890.

- Francois Eloury, 1773
Pourquier factory

After leaving the Grande Maison, François Eloury established the second faïencerie in Quimper sometime between 1773 and 1776. There is some disagreement on the exact date. Eloury's son Guillaume succeeded his father and Guillaume's son-in-law, Charles Porquier, succeeded Guillaume as director of the faïencerie. When Porquier assumed the directorship, the faïencerie took the name "Eloury-Pourquier". In 1838, at the young age of twenty-seven, Porquier's son Auguste assumed the directorship and began to expand the factory. By 1869, under the direction of Auguste Porquier, aided by his son Adolphe, the Porquier faïencerie was producing large quantities of a variety of wares. The "AP" mark was introduced by Adolphe at about this time, however it was seldom used until it was registered in 1897. Wares bearing this "AP" mark are quite rare and are sought after by collectors.

Following Adolphe's death, his widow hired Alfred Beau, a noted artist from Morlaix. Beau's arrival in Quimper in 1872 signaled the beginning of the Golden Age of the faïence of Quimper and especially for the wares produced by the factory which was now known as the "Porquier" faïencerie. The Porquier faïencerie began using the linked "PB" mark in 1875 although it was not registered until 1898.

Alfred Beau was an artist of the first order. His exquisite *Scenes Bretonnes* series depicts everyday Breton life. His *Botanique* series, featuring flora and fauna, is spectacular. Alfred Beau also designed the *Legendes Bretonnes* series illustrating the legends of Brittany. Beau's artwork graced a variety of forms, from a simple dinner plate or platter to

Marked "Dieppe" on the front, this vividly decorated mug was probably made to be sold as a souvenir in Dieppe. Signed on the bottom "PB". The Porquier faïencerie produced everyday wares along with the magnificent wares designed by Alfred Beau. 4 1/2" tall, c.1904.

an intricately molded inkwell or *bonbonière*. Because of the exceptional quality of Beau's designs, colors and forms, these wares are Quimper's very best and are treasured by collectors today just as one would treasure a masterpiece on canvas.

Despite faïence's great popularity and Beau's artistry, financial difficulties beset the Porquier factory toward the end of the nineteenth century. In 1903 Beau resigned. The "PB" mark would no longer be used. Arthur Porquier managed the faïencerie, sometimes marking his wares "AP", until its demise in 1904 or 1905.

Scene of Breton children at play adorns this *mouchoir* or handkerchief produced by the Porquier faïencerie. Blue on blue *décor riche* border and a blue bow at the top adorn this exquisite piece. 11" long, 5" wide, 4 1/2" tall, PB, c.1890.

Alfred Beau designed a series of *Legendes Bretonne*. This example is titled *Yann Coz chez les Diables*, that is, *Old Jean in the house of the Devils*. Bold and dramatic! 9 3/4" diameter, PB, c.1890.

A green on yellow *décor riche* border bearing the coat of arms of Brittany decorates this plate titled "Roscoff" (a seaside town in Brittany). 9 3/4" diameter, PB, c.1890.

Blue on yellow *décor riche* border with the coat of arms of Brittany border this delightful scene from the Porquier faïencerie. Perhaps this Breton couple is returning from the market with their dinner. 9 3/4" diameter, PB, c.1890.

This spectacular vase features a beautifully painted scene of Breton musicians and dancers on the front, and a delicate geranium spray on the back. Two small chips on the back of the base do not impair the integrity of this museum quality piece. Signed "PB Banalec", 12" tall by 15" wide, 19th century.

Deeply scalloped bowl from the Porquier faïencerie. Soft blue morning glories. 8 1/4" diameter, PB, c.1890

Vivid yellows and blues dominate the geometric décor of this small pitcher produced in the Porquier faïencerie. 4" tall, c.1904.

A rare find! A tea or coffee service complete
with tray. The ensemble speaks for itself.
AP, c.1900.

The *fleur de lys* is the symbol of France and here it is a wonderful place card holder, edged in blue and unmarked but certainly AP production. 3 1/2" tall, c.1900.

An exquisite 9 1/4" diameter plate, slightly tinged with blue, from Alfred Beau's *Botanique* series. Unmarked, professional restoration, c.1880.

This unmarked 9" diameter plate is 19th
century production. The *coiffe* and narrow
waist of the Bretonne are indicative of AP
figures. c.1895.

Fleur de lys place card holder, also
unmarked but surely AP. 3" tall, c.1900.

An exquisite example of a masterpiece in faïence from the HR faïencerie! Lovely scene of children playing marbles . A village in the background. Private collection. 10 3/4" long, 8" wide, HR, c.1895.

A wonderfully large platter with a Bretonne figure and vivid yellow and orange *a la touche* border décor. Henriot Q, 9 3/4" wide and 15" long, c.1935.

- Guillaume Dumaine, 1778 Henriot factory

The Henriot faïencerie was founded in 1778 by Guillaume Dumaine, a young man from Normandy. Dumaine's production consisted mainly of utilitarian stoneware or *Grès*, usually undecorated, occasionally decorated in a simple and primitive manner. Dumaine's faïencerie was managed by succeeding generations, employing only a few people until, more than one hundred years later, in 1884, Jules Henriot, at the tender age of 18, assumed the management of the family business that would bear his name for many years.

Soon after Jules assumed the directorship of the faïencerie, he instituted his first mark, "HR". The "H" is for Henriot and the "R" is for his wife's maiden name. Jules Henriot's skillful management of the faïencerie and the increasing popularity of Quimper ware, led to the great success of the Henriot factory at this time. Henriot expanded the faïencerie and produced wares that captured the charm of Brittany. The *Petit Breton* style had taken shape and a *petite pièce de faïence* was the perfect souvenir of a pleasant summer sojourn in Brittany.

In 1913, Henriot exhibited a stroke of genius--he purchased the designs, molds and marks of the now defunct Porquier factory. Alfred Beau's magnificent designs were re-issued by Henriot from 1913 to 1930, bearing the mark "PB Quimper" while even later editions were signed "Henriot, Quimper".

There is a distinct difference in color between Beau's original wares and the re-editions. The wares produced by the Porquier faïencerie have a lovely, faint bluish tinge while the wares produced after 1913 by the Henriot faïencerie have a creamy or occasionally pinkish tinge to the glaze.

These two pitchers are superb examples of *croisillé* décor. The top of each pitcher bears a red lattice design bordered in blue, the center bears a blue and red lattice and dot design and panels with finely detailed peasants. Just above the base there is a swag and tassel border. The pitcher on the bottom has a ladybug applied to the center panel! Bottom: 8 1/2" tall, Top: 5 3/4" tall, both marked Henriot Q, c.1930-35.

1922 was a landmark year for the Henriot factory. The Grande Maison HB filed suit accusing the Henriot faïencerie of trademark infringement, claiming that the linked letters "HR" were easily mistaken for their "HB". The Grande Maison prevailed and Jules Henriot was directed to change his mark. Henriot chose to sign his wares "HenRiot". By capitalizing both the "H" and the "R", the mark emphasized the original "HR" mark. Few dates concerning the history of the marks used by the faïenceries of Quimper can be so precisely set as this one.

Disaster struck in 1925 when the faïencerie was destroyed by fire. Undaunted, Jules Henriot turned this disaster into an opportunity, constructing a larger building and modernizing production methods. While production of the many patterns featuring the Breton peasant continued, wares in the Art Deco or Modern Movement style were added to Henriot's ever expanding repertoire.

Henriot retired in 1946 leaving the business to succeeding generations. In 1968, just as financial difficulties beset the firm, the city of Quimper proposed a road project that would require the demolition of the Henriot faïencerie. This was a mixed blessing; it became the catalyst for the merger of Quimper's two remaining faïenceries.

The Grande Maison expanded its facilities and in moved the Henriot workers. For the next fifteen years the HB and Henriot faïenceries shared one plant but remained separate, that is, each produced their own designs and signed their wares accordingly. Regretfully, in 1983 financial and labor problems forced both factories into bankruptcy. The following year Sarah and Paul Janssens, the importers of Quimper ware to the United States, bought the ailing company and production continues today.

Rectangular platter with cut corners is bordered with *a la touche* sprays and black ermine tails while the *sujet ordinaire* is flanked with *demi-fantaisie* florals. 9 1/2" long, 6 1/2" wide, Henriot Q, c.1935-40.

This lovely *bannette* or two handled tray features a finely drawn Breton couple and a lovely *demi-fantaisie* border. 8" wide, 12 1/2" long, HRQ, c.1915.

A dramatic platter in the *Ivoire Corbeille* décor features a gay procession of Bretons led by two musicians. Henriot Q, 10" wide, 20" long, c.1935.

Souvenir pieces were produced for many towns and villages and often were marked with the name of the town or village where they were to be sold. This generously sized rippled bowl, from *Luc sur Mer* bears the popular *sujet ordinaire* décor. 11" diameter, Henriot Q, c.1925.

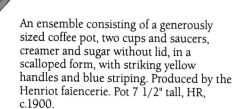

An ensemble consisting of a generously sized coffee pot, two cups and saucers, creamer and sugar without lid, in a scalloped form, with striking yellow handles and blue striping. Produced by the Henriot faïencerie. Pot 7 1/2" tall, HR, c.1900.

Trefoil server with a lovely blue scallop and dot border. The arched handle is 5 1/2" tall, 11" long and 11" wide, Henriot Q, c.1935-40.

This diminutive teapot and *sucrier* or sugar feature finely rendered Bretons in a central medallion, delicate décor all around. A sweet little pair. Henriot Q, c.1930.

This truly lovely pen tray features a Breton musician, flanked by *demi-fantaisie* sprays. The scallop shells and *fleurs de lys* are painted in lovely blues. 5" wide, 11" long, HRQ, c.1910.

This deeply scalloped bowl was produced by the Henriot faïencerie from a mold purchased from the Porquier faïencerie. A lovely lady carrying a basket has her back to us, an unusual pose. The border pattern is delicate and lacy. 8 1/4" diameter, Henriot Q, c.1925,.

For *pétit déjeuner* or breakfast, an oversized rippled cup for Marcel's coffee on a beautifully decorated, oversized saucer with a place for his croissant. A wonderful way to start the day! The figures are finely drawn and the floral sprays are delicate. The finely worked *croisillé* pattern and scallop shells are lovely. Altogether, a rare beauty. Henriot Q, c.1925-30.

Another *petit dejeuner* set in a similar form; this is decorated with scallop shells in cobalt blue and gold. Marked with a large, impressive, blue "HR Quimper", saucer 6 1/2" wide, 11" long, cup 4 1/2" diameter, c.1910.

A pair of small bowls featuring a finely drawn and colorfully dressed Breton couple. 2" high, 4 1/2" diameter, Henriot Q, c.1940.

Vivid yellow and blue adorn these whimsical little fish for your salt. 2 1/2" wide, 4 1/2" long, Henriot Q, c.1935-40.

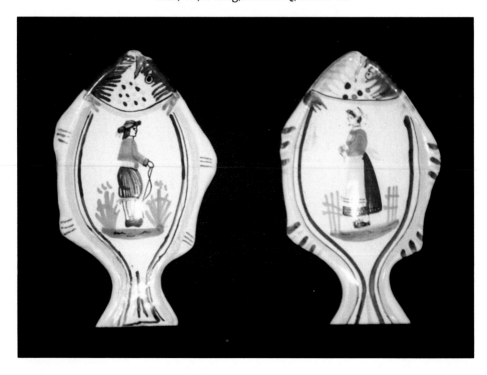

This stately Breton couple is clad in the deep blue and gold favored in Brittany. 9 1/2" tall, Henriot Q, c.1935.

A petite Bretonne on her way to market! Vivid color. 3 3/4" tall, Henriot Q, c.1935-40.

Croisillé décor at its best on this little covered *boite.* 3 1/2" diameter, 2" tall, Henriot Q, c.1930.

A marvelous pair of
vases in the ever
popular *biniou* or
bagpipe form. Beauti-
fully rendered in great
detail. A pair of
musicians play for a
handsome dancing
couple. 7 1/2" tall,
HRQ, c.1910.

The back of the vases
in the previous photo
bear the coat of arms of
Brittany.

A sweet pair of pots for salt or jam. 1 1/2"
tall, 2 1/2" diameter, HRQ, C 1915.

A *demi-fantaisie* plate, beautifully executed
in vivid colors. The yellow apron and jug
draw the eye to a lovely Bretonne. 9 1/2"
diameter, HRQ, c.1910.

A heart shaped *tulipière* featuring a strolling gentleman from Normandy. An especially colorful and important piece marked only *"Bernieres sur Mer"*, as a souvenir. 10" tall, 9 1/2" wide, c.1930.

Quintal with a finely rendered Breton playing his *bombarde*. Banded in the middle with an interesting zigzag pattern. 5 3/4" tall, Henriot Q, c.1930.

A *petit* version of the vase in the following photo. 5" tall, c.1935.

A gracefully formed vase featuring a Bretonne in a colorful costume bearing a water jug on her head. 8" tall, Henriot Q, c.1935.

This richly decorated ewer with a *décor riche* border, blue on blue around the spout, and blue on yellow below, complements a beautifully detailed scene of a Breton couple. A large and graceful handle. 16" tall, HRQ, c.1935.

❖ 59

This pair of vases has it all: form, color, and décor! 11 1/2" tall, Henriot Q, c.1935.

This square vase features a bagpipe player clad in cobalt blue and gold. The cut corners are decorated with touches of cobalt blue, ermine tails and a four red dot décor. Small chip on the base. 6 1/2" tall, 3 1/4" diameter, Henriot Q, c.1935.

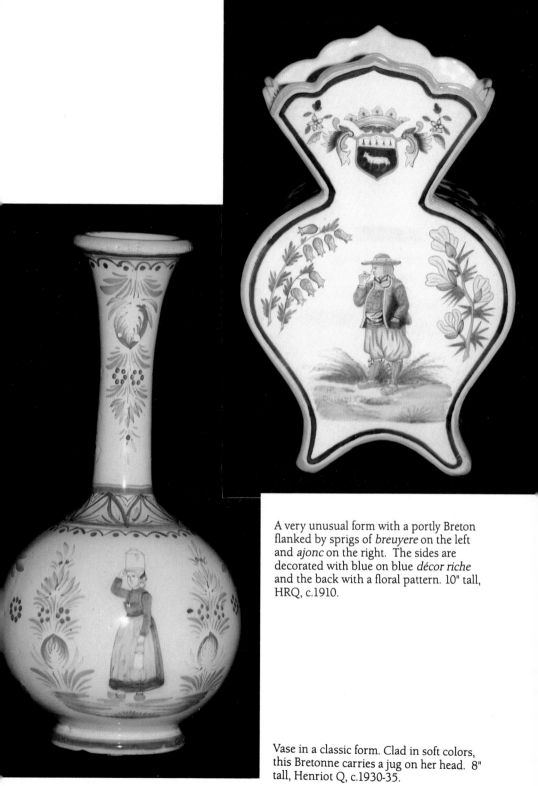

A very unusual form with a portly Breton flanked by sprigs of *breuyere* on the left and *ajonc* on the right. The sides are decorated with blue on blue *décor riche* and the back with a floral pattern. 10" tall, HRQ, c.1910.

Vase in a classic form. Clad in soft colors, this Bretonne carries a jug on her head. 8" tall, Henriot Q, c.1930-35.

A Bretonne taking time to smell the flowers adorns this little flower pot, scalloped rim, exquisite color. 2 1/2" tall, 3" diameter, HRQ, c. 1910.

Demi-fantaisie décor and a Bretonne in the *sujet ordinaire* style decorate this teapot with a cobalt blue sponged handle. 5 3/4" high, 5 3/4" wide, HRQ, c.1910.

Generously sized teapot in *demi-fantaisie* décor with a *sujet ordinaire* Bretonne. 7" tall, 8 1/2" across, HRQ, c.1910.

Yellow glazed wares were introduced in the 1920s. The teapot, creamer and two cups and saucers were produced about ten years later. The teapot is 7" tall and 10" from tip to tip. Henriot Q, c.1930.

Yellow bellows with *croisillé* décor and a *sujet ordinaire.* 7 1/2" long, 3 1/4" wide, Henriot Q, c.1940.

A demure *sujet ordinaire* graces this small banded jug. Note the shaky blue band at the top, always a reminder that each piece was painted by hand. 7" tall, Henriot Q, c.1935.

A snuff in the popular bagpipe form. *Sujet Ordinaire* with a yellow bow. 3" tall, 2 1/2 wide, HR, c.1900.

Another bagpipe ! This time a snuff featuring a Bretonne with a blue bow. 3" tall, 2 1/4" wide, unsigned, c. 1930.

The shape of the Breton gentleman seems to mirror the shape of this vase! Lovely detail on the unusual tassel shaped handles and around the top the vase. 12" tall, Henriot Q, c.1935-40.

A dramatic pair of plates with the *décor riche* border and *sujets varies*. The figures are clad in wonderfully colorful Breton costumes. The plate on the left bears the crest of Brittany; the plate on the right bears the coat of arms of Quimper. These re-editions of earlier PB and HR plates are more vividly colored and less expensive than their earlier counterparts. Expect to pay considerably more for earlier *décor riche* pieces. 10" diameter, Henriot Q, c.1940.

This striking *melonnier* is a dramatic piece, large and exquisitely decorated with a *décor riche* border encircling a charming couple on their way to market. The crest of Brittany at the top and the scallop shells on the handles are perfect finishing touches. A re-edition of an earlier pattern. 14" across the handles, Henriot Q, c.1935.

This splendid hexagonal cup and saucer in the *demi-fantaisie* décor shows a Breton couple in the now familiar *sujet ordinaire* manner. Each panel is outlined in cobalt. Saucer 5 1/2" diameter, cup 2 3/4" tall, Henriot Q, c.1935-40.

A *petite* scalloped cup and saucer in an adorable form! Cup is 2 3/4" diameter, the saucer is 4 1/4" diameter, HRQ, c. 1915.

A sweet square cup and saucer with cut corners, decorated with a *sujet ordinaire* and the *demi-fantaisie* border décor. Cup is 2 1/4" tall and 2 1/2" square while the saucer is 4 3/4" diameter, Henriot Q, c.1930.

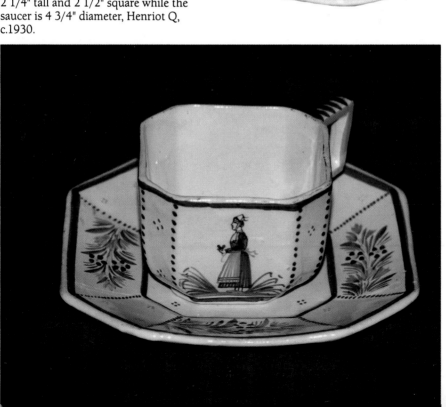

This lovely pair of wall pockets is decorated with *sujets ordinaires*, ermine tails, and flowers. 6 1/2" long, HRQ, c. 1915.

Perhaps this is a paperweight. It has no opening for snuff or flowers. Quite unusual. Marked only "Quimper, Made in France" but probably produced by the Henriot factory to be sold as a souvenir in Quimper. 3 1/2" tall and 2" wide, c.1925.

A small pitcher to accompany the cup and saucer in the previous photo. 4" tall and 5" across the handle, Henriot Q, c.1935-40.

Chamber stick decorated in the naive manner. 6" diameter, 2 1/2" tall. Soft colors, glaze drips on the bottom. Henriot Q, c.1935.

The cobalt décor on this chamber stick is striking! The flower pattern is applied with a sponge. 5" diameter, unmarked but surely an Henriot piece, c.1925-30.

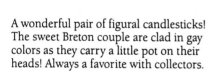

A wonderful pair of figural candlesticks!
The sweet Breton couple are clad in gay
colors as they carry a little pot on their
heads! Always a favorite with collectors.

This single candlestick is gracefully shaped
and decorated with sprigs of flowers, a
Breton peasant, and cobalt blue highlights.
8" tall, small chip on *bobeche*, Henriot Q,
c.1935.

A superb example of the *biniou* form! Pipe holder for four pipes is surmounted with a crown above a crest of black ermine tails. A beautifully rendered Breton couple sit above the holder for the pipes. 11" long, 6 1/2" tall, HRQ, c.1910.

This is a most unusual form for the popular *biniou*. A lovely blue bow and blue sponge work on the edge. The pipes form a raised handle and stylized flowers decorate the bowl. 8" long, Henriot Q, c.1935.

A closer look at the unusual handle on the bowl pictured above.

A magnificent swan 16" long and 7 1/2" tall
with six small swans to be used as egg
cups. Gracefully arched neck is decorated
with blue sponged circles around orange
circles. Lovely multi-colored tail feathers.
An imposing piece! Henriot Q, c.1935.

Sweet little dish for bonbons! Blue sponged handles topped with a yellow and red applied flower. Stylized blue and orange flowers inside and out. 5" diameter, Henriot Q, c.1925.

Sweet 4 1/2" tall pitcher bearing a Breton flanked by *demi-fantaisie arbustes.* HRQ, c.1910-15.

This 8" tall pedestal base jug is a classic. A *sujet ordinaire* Breton is flanked by floral sprays and banded in yellow and blue. Henriot Q, c.1940.

This 3 1/2" rippled creamer is exquisite!
The handle is especially lovely. Decorated
with two-toned blue *fleurs de lys* and black
ermine tails. HRQ, 3" tall, c.1910.

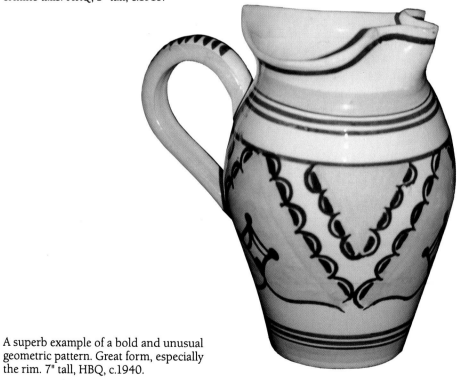

A superb example of a bold and unusual
geometric pattern. Great form, especially
the rim. 7" tall, HBQ, c.1940.

Dragon handled wares are in great demand. This pitcher is a dear. 3 3/8" tall, Henriot Q, c.1930.

Bruyeres decorate a little pitcher banded in gold and green. 4 1/2" tall, Henriot Q, c.1940-45.

Ménagère in a delightful form with *demi-fantaisie* florals. The heart and spade on either side hold salt and pepper while the center section holds mustard. 5" long, 3" tall, Henriot Q, c.1930.

A tall, handsome jug, an unusual form with bold colors! 9 1/2" tall, Henriot Q, c.1940.

The artist's palette to hang and fill with flowers. A rare treasure. 8 1/2" tall, 7" wide, marked only "France", c.1935.

A treasure! This *jardinière* with gargoyle feet is beautifully decorated. The Breton man in his gaily colored costume strikes a casual pose for his demure lady. 10" long, 6" tall, HRQ, c.1910.

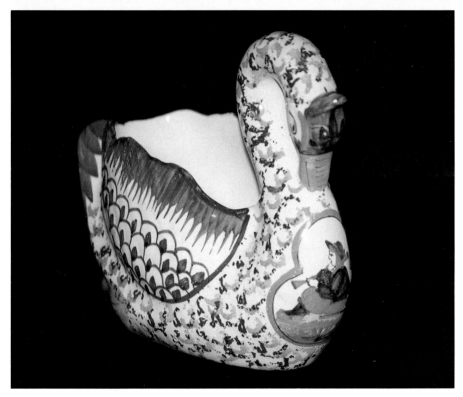

A bagpipe player adorns this swan *jardinière* decorated in blue and gold sponging with stylized blue feathers. 6 1/2" tall, 8" long, Henriot Q, c.1935.

Swans are a popular form in the faïenceries of Quimper and here a pair of swans form the *jardinière* while their arched necks create a handle. 9" tall and 9" wide, Henriot Q, c.1945.

A charming young man plays his *bombarde* for a sweet young lady. This wonderful *jardinière* is 14 1/2" long and 6" tall. Henriot Q, c.1930.

The form of this 4" tall and 6" wide fan-shaped vase is delightful. The geometric décor and the blue sponged feet are most pleasing. The colors are soft and delicate. The lady is presented in the *sujet ordinaire* manner. HRQ, c.1915.

This fan-shaped vase, also in the *sujet ordinaire* manner, marked Henriot Quimper, is the same size as the fan in the previous photo but was produced later and is therefore slightly less expensive. 6" tall and 6" wide, HRQ. c. 1940.

Another version of the fan-shaped vase. Henriot Q c.1935.

Beautifully decorated pair of vases filled
with black-eyed susans. Gold and cobalt
blue geometric bands ring the top and
bottom. Carefully rendered figures. 8" tall,
Henriot Q, c.1930.

The form, color and décor of this vase are exquisite! The cobalt blue trim is deep and vivid. The Bretonne is carefully rendered with an eye-catching yellow apron and basket. A splendid form. 8 1/2" tall, HRQ, c.1915.

The elegant vase is decorated with cobalt blue and gold geometric and floral sprays on either side of the detailed yet naive lady who holds a staff and spins flax. 12 1/2" tall, Henriot Q, top of right handle has been restored, c.1935.

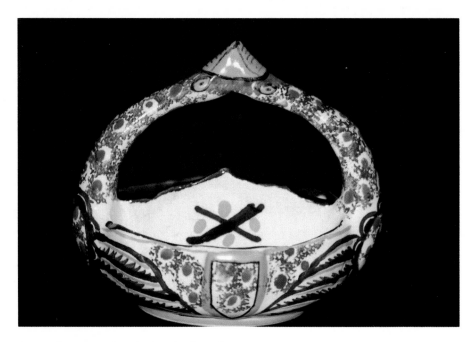

A pair of swans with arched necks form the
handle for little salt. 3 1/4" wide, 4" tall,
Henriot Q, c.1940-45.

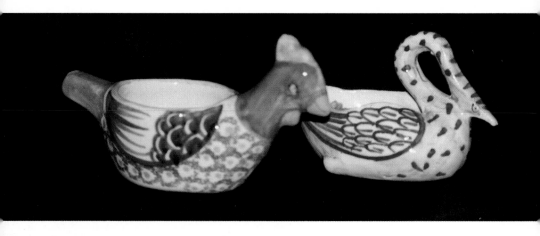

On the left: a rooster for your morning egg
is decorated with blue sponge circles
around rosy dots. 4" long, Henriot Q,
c.1940. On the right: a very graceful swan
for salt. 4" long, HR, c.1903.

Swans for your salt! The interiors are decorated one with a man and one with a woman, 4" long, left is marked HRQ, c.1910, right is marked Henriot Q, c. 1935-40.

Quintal or five fingered vase, featuring a man in the costume of Normandy. Tiny flake on center finger. 5 1/2" tall, marked only as a souvenir from "Lisieux", c.1935-40.

Charming little footed ink pot bordered in cobalt blue with a naively rendered Breton couple and *croisillé* panels on the sides. 4" tall, Henriot Q, c.1925.

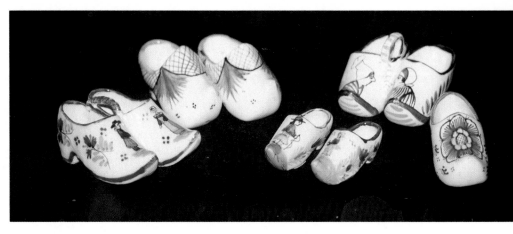

An assortment of wooden shoes. Left to right: Pair joined with twisted handle, detailed in next photo. Two shoes with red *croisillé* and blue accents, no mark, c.1930. Pair joined with yellow striped handle, portrait bust of figure on each, 3" long, HBQ, c.1935. Single shoe with wonderful blue blossom, no mark, 3" long. In the foreground, a pair in miniature, no mark, 2" long, c. 1930.

Pair of shoes outlined in blue and decorated with vivid cobalt blue flowers and four dot design. Notice the unevenness of the outline and the imperfect spot of glaze on the right shoe, all are indicators of age. Newer pieces will not have these irregularities. *Sujet ordinaire* on each. Marked as a souvenir "St. Brieuc", 3" long, c.1930

Egg cup on the left is decorated in the *Ivoire Corbeille* pattern and features a Bretonne lady. On the right, a pair of egg cups, a man and lady, with *a la touche* décor and four dot design in red and blue. All marked Henriot Q, 3 1/2" tall, c.1935.

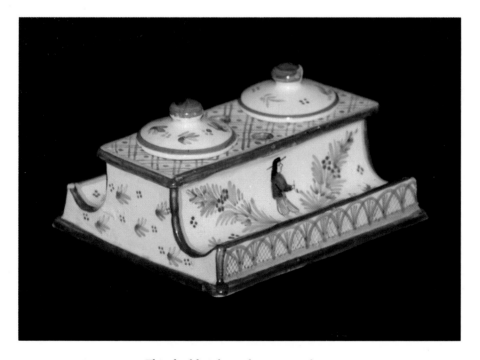

This double inkstand is exquisitely decorated with red *croisillé*, cobalt blue trim, and soft florals with a man on one side and a lady on the other. 5" wide, 6" long and 2" tall, HRQ, c.1915.

A splendid form! The inkwell rests inside four richly colored *fleurs de lys*. The base is footed, bordered in cobalt blue, and trimmed with a red scroll and dot pattern. Truly a gem. 4" tall, 3" square, HRQ, c.1910.

Each of these inkwells has a sweet form! The castle turret on the left is 3" tall, 3 3/4" square, HRQ, c.1920. The star shaped inkwell is footed and bears a naive yet detailed lady. There is a small chip on the lid. 3 1/2" tall, 4" wide, HRQ, c.1920. The round ink pot has a base with a rolled pie crust edge sponged in green. The Bretonne lady is seated between green bushes. 3 1/2" tall, base 5" diameter, HRQ, c.1915-20.

A sweet crescent shaped double inkwell featuring a bagpipe player. Sides and back are rippled! Blue striping outlines the piece. Henriot Q, 6" long, c.1935.

An early Henriot plate decorated with *gros filets*, that is, concentric yellow and blue bands on the border and 4 "tennis balls" around a center panel of red and blue *croisillé*. Henriot Q, 7" diameter, c.1925.

Croisillé décor is exquisite and very popular with collectors. This wonderful handled 13" cake plate features two musicians, one playing the *biniou* and the other playing the *bombarde*. Red and blue *croisillé* panels alternate with panels bearing one stylized flower. Scalloped rim. Henriot Q, c.1945.

This 9 1/2" plate in the same décor as the plate in the previous photo features a debonair Breton clad in a cobalt blue jacket and yellow pants. Henriot Q, c.1935.

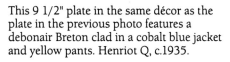

Lovely 9" plate in the same décor with slightly scalloped rim and a Bretonne holding a distaff for spinning flax. Henriot Q, c.1935.

A lovely bird and dragonfly meet on this plate in the *Botanique* series designed by Alfred Beau, signed PB Quimper. The addition of the word "Quimper" to the PB mark indicates that the piece was produced by the Henriot faïencerie between 1913-1930. 9 1/2" diameter, PBQ.

The border pattern of alternating panels with sprays of *ajonc* and *bruyere* decorate this 9 3/4" plate featuring two musicians and the crest of Brittany. Henriot Q, c.1930.

The rippled and scalloped border on the 11" charger is decorated in the *a la touche* manner. The naively painted lady is holding a flower. Henriot Q, c.1945.

The same Bretonne carrying the yellow jug is shown on page 51. Here she is surrounded by garlands in the *demi-fantaisie* pattern on a plate with folded sides sponged in blue. 8 1/2" diameter, HRQ, c.1910.

This pair of scallop shells has an early, naive charm. Gold bows adorn each shell, one bearing a Breton man in cobalt blue *bragoubraz* and yellow knee socks, the other a lady in a cobalt blue skirt and red apron.
Demi-fantaisie florals. 6 1/2" by 7", HRQ, c.1905-10.

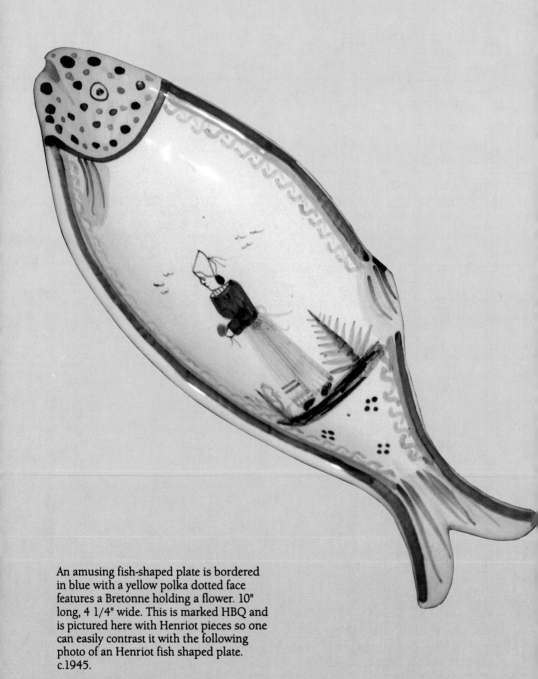

An amusing fish-shaped plate is bordered
in blue with a yellow polka dotted face
features a Bretonne holding a flower. 10"
long, 4 1/4" wide. This is marked HBQ and
is pictured here with Henriot pieces so one
can easily contrast it with the following
photo of an Henriot fish shaped plate.
c.1945.

Considerably more detailed and earlier than the previous plate. The fish has a blue polka dotted face and bears a carefully drawn lady carrying one jug on her head and another in her hand. The colors of her pink apron and cobalt blue skirt are lovely. 10" long, 4 1/4" wide, Henriot Q, c.1930.

A portrait of George Washington decorates this 10" long fish shaped plate from the Grande Maison. Probably produced in limited quantity for a special occasion. 10" long, 4 1/4" wide, HBQ, c.1945.

Square plate with cut
corners is 8" and
marked Henriot Q. The
Bretonne is flanked by
a la touche florals. All
rendered in soft colors,
c.1930.

This version of the
square plate features a
Breton. Yellow has been
added to the border
décor. 8", Henriot Q,
c.1930.

This is a slightly later example of the same square plate. This series of three photos illustrates that one must handle and examine carefully the wares, as often as possible, to gain a knowledge of the characteristics of different periods of production. Henriot Q, c.1940.

Fluid lines and soft colors combine with black ermine tails and a Breton lady to make an altogether lovely square bowl. Very naive in character. 8" square, Henriot Q, c.1925.

Tea tile is bordered in a green chain pattern and the corners, decorated in *demi-fantaisie* florals, gently curve upward. A Breton musician is nicely rendered. 7" square, HRQ, c.1910.

This cheese plate has a wonderful star shape and a very large cover. Bordered in the *demi-fantaisie* pattern, the cover features a naively drawn Breton couple and a green sponged handle. There is a small chip on the underside of the plate and a small gouge on the upper edge of the underplate (visible in the photo on the back, left edge). 11" diameter underplate, 4" tall, Henriot Q, c.1930.

Server divided into six squares and trimmed with blue sponging. Generously sized. 8 3/4" wide, 14 3/4" long Henriot Q, c.1940.

A covered cheese dish similar in form to the one at left, but smaller. Plate 8 1/2" diameter, lid 6" diameter, 2 1/2" tall, Henriot Q, c.1935.

A magnificent covered butter in the *biniou* form. Blue on blue *décor riche* borders the cover which features a seated Breton playing his horn. Floral sprays of *ajonc* and *bruyere* decorate both the lid and the underplate. The pipes on the lid are raised to function as a handle. 11" long and 8" wide, Henriot Q, c.1935.

The form and décor on this covered cheese dish are spectacular. The photo says it all. 8" diameter, HRQ, c.1915.

This little hexagonal teapot is decorated in the *demi-fantaisie* pattern and bears a *sujet ordinaire* in the naive manner. 6" tall and 6" handle to spout, HRQ, c.1910.

Splendid form for the covered butter dish. Shaped like a six pointed star, there are holes pierced in the underplate. *Fleur de lys* finial. 7" diameter, Henriot, c.1935.

Three pieces featuring the Mayflower flying the French flag. Left to Right: *Biberon* marked "PV" in a circle and "France", 4" tall, c.1935. *Quintal,* or five-fingered vase, marked Henriot Q, 3 1/2" tall, c.1935. Match holder bordered in red and gold, 2 1/4" tall, also marked "PV" in a circle, c.1935.

This holder, made for Camel cigarettes, is a very rare and sought-after piece. Chip on top, left corner. 3" tall, 3" long, Henriot Q, c.1935.

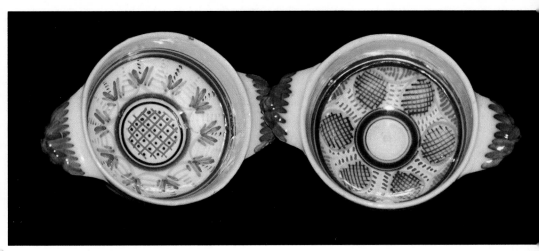

Two fine examples of geometric décor! On the left red and blue *croisillé* and dot pattern with stylized flowers and on the right the "tennis" pattern. 5" diameter, unmarked but surely from the Henriot faïencerie, c.1910.

Match holder, pierced to hang, is decorated with floral sprays and a *sujet ordinaire* (Bretonne), 3 1/4" tall, HRQ, c.1915-20.

A delightful little mustard pot with blue scallop and dot border on the base bears a *sujet ordinaire* on the pot. 3 1/2" tall, Henriot Q, c.1935.

Two menus, both bordered in cobalt blue and bearing the crest of Brittany. Each *porte-menu* bears a *sujet varié*. 5" tall, 3 1/2" wide, HRQ, c.1910.

A winsome Breton couple done in a *petit* size. He plays the *biniou* and she carries her umbrella. 4" tall, Henriot Q, c.1925.

Bretonne lady wears a tall *coiffe* and a pink apron over her cobalt blue skirt. This is a bank with a slot for coins in the back and a lock on the bottom. Quite unusual. 5" tall, Henriot Q, c.1930.

This jug is called a *biberon*– used as baby bottles in the nineteenth century. A lovely form. 6" tall, Henriot Q, c.1940.

Another *biberon* with uneven white glaze and soft, delicate colors. There is also a handle in the back! Look carefully at this photo. You will see glaze skips and a smudge of paint, both of which help to date the piece. 8" tall, Henriot Q, c.1925.

This spectacular *soupière* is in pristine condition. A naively rendered lady is surrounded by a *demi-fantaisie* border on the lid. The green, yellow and red *a la touche* pattern on the bowl is especially lovely. Blue and yellow bands. A large and important piece. The lid is 18" in diameter while the entire piece is 9" tall! HRQ, c.1910-20.

A mug for cider or coffee decorated with a naively drawn Breton and *demi-fantaisie* florals. 3" tall, Henriot Q, c.1935.

"Annaik" is 3 1/2" tall and and probably going to market with her basket. Right front of base is restored. Henriot Q, c.1930.

Three *biberons* of various sizes and periods. Left: 6 1/2" tall, Henriot Q, c.1940. Center: pinkish cast from the red clay, 4 1/2" tall, Henriot Q, c.1925. Right: 6 1/2" tall, Henriot Q, c.1930-35.

Oval plate features a Bretonne with a cobalt blue skirt and pink apron. She is flanked by floral sprays. Bordered in blue and gold bands and a four red dot pattern. 6" long, 3 1/2" wide, Henriot Q, c.1940.

Workers in the faïencerie, c. 1875.

Chapter 3

A CLOSE LOOK AT THE POTTERY WARES

- Marks

In the eighteenth century, the faïenceries of Quimper seldom marked their wares. It was not until the second half of the nineteenth century, sometime between 1860 and 1870, that the Grande Maison first marked their wares with an "HB", though this mark was not registered until 1882. The marks most commonly used by the three faïenceries are listed here:

The Grande Maison HB

Used from 1860 or 1870 to 1883, registered 1882

The Grande Maison's first mark (note the tail on the B) was registered in 1882. Very rare!

Used and registered 1883 to 1904

The Grande Maison's second mark, "HB" (without the tail), was registered in 1883 and used until 1904.

Used from 1904 - 1968

The "HB Quimper" mark was used by the Grande Maison from 1904 until 1968 and, occasionally, from 1968 to 1983.

Registered in 1922, probably used until the 1940s

The "HB Odetta, Quimper" mark - registered in 1922 and used until sometime in the early 1940s.

1939, used on wares produced for the Hotel de l'Epée in Quimper

The rare and unusual mark of the fish of St. Corentin was used on wares produced for the Hotel de l'Epée in Quimper in 1939.

Registered 1943, used from 1943 to 1968

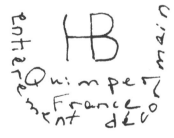

1968 - 1983

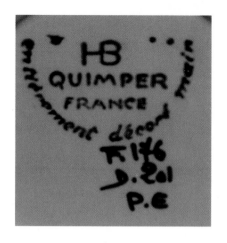

From 1968 to 1983 this mark was stamped on the wares by both the Grande Maison and the Henriot faïencerie (simply replacing the HB with Henriot).

Current Marks

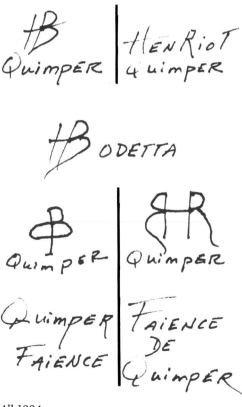

All 1984

1984 to present

The Porquier-Beau mark, registered in 1898, in use from 1875. Often accompanied by the title of the scene or pattern (Banalec).

The Porquier Faïencerie

Extremely rare, about 1845

Used from 1875 to 1904, registered 1898.

Adolphe Porquier's mark, registered in 1898, in use from 1875.

Registered 1898, used until 1904

Used from 1875 to 1904, registered 1898

The Henriot Faïencerie

Registered 1904, used earlier and until 1904

The first mark of the Henriot faïencerie was used during the last quarter of the nineteenth century, although not registered until 1904.

Used between 1913 and 1930

The "PB Quimper" mark is a mark of the Henriot faïencerie! The PB molds, patterns and marks were purchased by the Maison Henriot in 1913. Re-issues bear the original "PB" to denote their origin and "Quimper" to distinguish them from the original Porquier wares.

1922 - 1968 The use of upper and lower case letters varies widely.

1904 - 1922

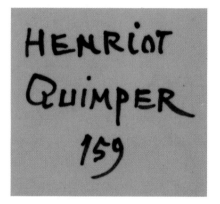

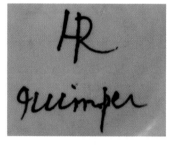

The faïenceries of Quimper added the word "Quimper" to all of their marks in 1904 to distinguish their wares from those of imitators in other parts of France.

The "HR" mark was changed to "HenRiot Quimper" in 1922 in response to legal action of the Grande Maison protesting the similarity of the two marks. Two more examples of this new mark follow.

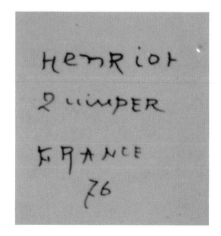

The "HR Quimper" mark in a different script. The marks were often written in several different scripts.

The "HenRiot Quimper" mark.

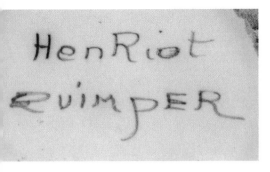

The "HenRiot Quimper" mark.

1968 - 1984

Current mark.

To review, there are two very significant and precise dates in the chronology of marks used by the Quimper faïenceries. First, in 1904 the word "Quimper" was added to all the marks of the faïenceries in Quimper in an attempt to clearly identify the wares from Quimper and to discourage the production of imitations being produced elsewhere in France. Then, in 1922, in the action initiated by the Grande Maison, the court directed the Henriot Faïencerie to change its mark, ruling that its "HR" signature too closely resembled the "HB" of the Grande Maison. No other dates in the chronology of the marks used by the faïenceries of Quimper ware can be set as precisely.

It is important to note that the location of a mark on a particular piece has no significance. Wares were marked inside, outside, front, back, bottom or top.

Soon after World War I, the faïenceries added the word "France" to the mark on wares made for export. Nevertheless, some of the pieces destined for the domestic market may have been marked with the word "France" and many pieces which were not marked "France" were certainly purchased in France and carried home by a visitor from another country. Thus, the presence of the word "France" with any Quimper mark, definitively indicates a piece produced after World War I but the absence of the word "France" does not necessarily indicate pre-World War I production.

❖ 113

- Dating Quimper wares

You will find it very difficult to date some wares. Handle and examine the wares as often as possible because this hands-on experience will be your most valuable education.

The following time periods are general guidelines when dating Quimper wares:

1850 - 1904

1904 - 1922

1922 - 1940

1940 - 1946*

1946 - 1968

1968 - 1984

Current production

*During World War II, production at the faïenceries was very limited, and most of the wares produced were for the German market.

- Decorations

Quimper's three faïenceries decorated their wares with an incredible variety of patterns, some of which were used for only a limited time while others were used for many years. Some of the most popular patterns used between 1875 and 1940 are described below.

Overall designs which encompass the entire piece:

Florals–Alfred Beau's *Botanique* series

Alfred Beau's superb *Botanique* series has an overall pattern with a narrow yellow rim. 9 1/2" diameter, Henriot Q, c.1915.

Bleuet–randomly placed blue sprigs
with a touch of green and sometimes red

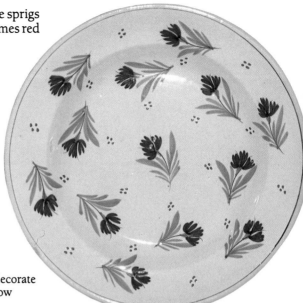

Bleuets and a four red dot pattern decorate
this 9 1/2" plate. Also a narrow yellow
border. Henriot Q, c.1930.

Ivoire Corbeille–red dots circled in
sponged blue with red touches forming
half of a floral blossom. All over a tan
glaze.

The *Ivoire Corbeille* pattern on this
bonbonière surrounds a portrait bust but
is often an overall pattern, omitting the
bust. 5" diameter. Henriot Q, c.1935.

Lys–the *fleur de lys*, the symbol of France, usually in two shades of blue

The symbol of France, the *fleur de lys* decorates this pitcher, banded in blue. 5" tall, Henriot Q.

Central designs:

Birds–a variety, but especially the very French symbol, the *Coq*

The *coq*, or rooster is painted in a vivid blue. Shape of the rim is lovely. 5" tall. Henriot Q, c. 1935.

Stylized bird adorns this plate with *gros filets* or yellow and blue concentric circles on the rim. 7" diameter, HRQ, c. 1910.

Basket of Flowers-- endless variations

Basket of flowers pattern in cobalt blue and soft red, yellow and green. A lovely early Henriot plate. 9 1/2" diameter, Henriot Q, c. 1925.

Geometric–let your imagination be your guide, dots, dashes, criss-cross, a limitless combination, sometimes with a smiling face in the center.

Geometrics are very popular and this 7" diameter plate is done in rich, vivid colors. Henriot Q, c.1935.

Petit Breton--some of the more
popular renditions are:

Sujet Ordinaire or Breton

The classic décor, a *sujet ordinaire* with
gros filets. Look carefully at each plate. The
one on the left is marked "Henriot,
Quimper" and the one on the right is
marked "HR Quimper". Notice that the
blue in the earlier "HR" plate "flows", a
characteristic of some of Henriot's c.1900
to 1925 production. The "Henriot" plate
has some of the characteristics of the
wares produced by the Henriot faïencerie.
c.1925 to 1935. Left: 8" diameter, Henriot
Q, c.1930; Right: 7" diameter, HRQ, c.1910.

Sujet Variés
Naive yet Detailed

Classic early "HB" naive, yet detailed décor on this 9" diameter plate. The Breton is clad in yellow *bragoubraz*, a cobalt blue jacket and pink shirt c. 1900.

Normandie

Normandie pattern features peasants clad in the typical costume of Normandy wearing large wooden shoes. The border décor seems to resemble seaweed! HBQ, 9 1/2", c.1930.

Bigouden

The *Bigoudén* pattern features Breton peasants in the manner of the modern movement, HBQ. 9 1/2", c. 1930.

Pecheur

Here the *Pecheur*, or fisherman pattern is decorated with fishing nets and a Bretonne waiting to fill her baskets with fish. HBQ, 9 1/2", c.1930.

The *Breton Broderie* décor frames a Breton couple on this bold platter. About 15" long, 8" wide, HBQ, c.1935.

Border designs:

Gros Filets–concentric yellow and blue bands

Gros Filets, the yellow and blue striped border, is the décor most commonly identified with Quimper ware. Here we see, on the left, an example from the Henriot faïencerie and on the right, the same pattern from the Grande Maison HB. Left: 8" diameter, c. 1930; Right: 8" diameter, c. 1935.

Décor Riche (also called *Rinceaux*)–acanthus leaves in two colors

The *décor riche* border from the Henriot faïencerie. Take a moment to look back at the same pattern from the Porquier and Grande Maison faïenceries and compare them with this one. 9 1/2", Henriot Q, c.1940.

Demi-fantaisie–floral garland and four dot pattern

This is a wonderful example of the *demi-fantaisie* border! The foliage is finely and generously drawn. HRQ, 9 1/2",

Croisillé–criss-cross pattern

The *croisillé* border décor is very appealing! There are some slight variations of this most popular pattern. Henriot Q, 9 1/2" diameter, c.1930.

Couronnes–floral garland

The Grande Maison was the originator of the *Couronnes* pattern and it is their most common and popular pattern. Also done in red and blue florals with green foliage. 6 1/2" wide, 8 1/2" long, HBQ, c.1935-40.

Festonné–repeated pattern of floral sprays, widely spaced, and four blue dots

Breton Broderie-stylized blue and gold pattern inspired by a popular embroidery pattern, 9 1/2" diameter, HBQ, c. 1940.

The *Breton Broderie* border pattern dates from the Art Deco era. 6" square, HBQ, c. 1925.

The Art Deco movement of the 1920s and 1930s influenced all of the arts and the faïence of Quimper was no exception. The Grande Maison embraced art deco with enthusiasm, introducing a line of *grès* ware, named "Odetta" for the River Odet which flows through Quimper. The masterful combination of angular and fluid lines in both form and décor resulted in some of the finest art pottery of the period. Odetta wares are highly prized by many French collectors while a small but enthusiastic number of American collectors focus on Odetta.

Odetta, the Art Deco line which derived its name from the Odet River, is *grès* ware. This compote is a lovely example of the exquisite combination of color and form that is typical of Odetta wares. About 5" tall, 6" diameter, HB Odetta Quimper, c.1920s.

The porringer is 7" in diameter, HB Odetta Quimper, c.1925-35.

126 ❖

Cider is a popular drink in Brittany. This attractive cider set has a large tray for the jug and six mugs. Tray is 12" diameter, pitcher is 8" tall, mugs are 3 3/4" tall, HB Odetta Quimper, c.1920s.

Covered *bonbonière* in three shades of blue is from the Odetta line. 5 1/4" diameter, 2 3/4" tall, HB Odetta Quimper, c.1920s.

A striking pitcher from the Odetta production of the Grande Maison. A Breton sailor and his lady, terrific color, 6" tall, HB Odetta, c. 1925.

This jug has a double spout, a form also popular with Native Americans. 5 1/2" across, 4 1/2" tall, HB Quimper Odetta, c.1925-30.

Odetta vase in the typical shades of brown with touches of white and cobalt blue. The band of figures is terrific! HBQ, c.1925-30.

During the same period, new artists were hired at both faïenceries and their work reflected the trends of the modern movement. A few of the most notable artists at the Grande Maison were Fouillen, Quillivic and Savigny. Paul Fouillen was hired as a painter in the early 1920s and soon became the Grande Maison's manager. In 1928 he opened his own faïencerie in Quimper. The décor of Fouillen's stoneware has decidedly Celtic roots. René Quillivic's sculpted wares are exquisite. Like Mary Cassat, Berthe Savigny of the Grande Maison is known for her figures of *bébés* and children.

Berthe Savigny created the mold for this figure of a young boy. Her figures of babies have the same sweet characteristics. 10" tall, HBQ, c.1930.

Paul Fouillen was associated with the Grande Maison until 1928 when he established his own faïencerie in Loc Maria. This 10" bowl, signed on the front and back, was produced in Fouillen's faïencerie. P Fouillen, c.1930.

Pair of bookends designed, produced and signed by "P. Fouillen". A demure couple in striking Breton costumes. Bookend on right has chip on base. 6" tall, 6" long, 1 1/2" wide, P. Fouillen Quimper, c.1930.

Meanwhile, the Henriot faïencerie was also adapting to the newest trends in the art world. Patterns and forms in the Art Deco style were introduced. Some of the most notable artists of the Henriot faïencerie were Bachelet, Maillard, Méheut, Nicot and Sevellec. Bachelet's sculptures are readily recognized because of their sharp, angular lines. Maillard is perhaps best known in the United States for his small, whimsical, reclining figures which serve as knife rests. Méheut designed many patterns with a marine motif but is widely known for the creation of an entire miniature Breton village. Nicot sculpted the "Three Gossips", perhaps the most well-known of all the figures produced in Quimper. Jim Sevellec was a very prolific artist, producing many small figures and a variety of dinnerware patterns. Sevellec also created a complete, miniature Breton village.

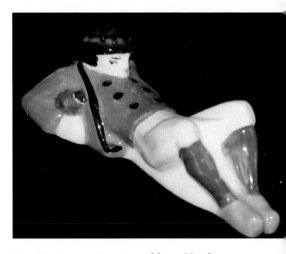

C.Maillard created a series of figural knife rests that are very popular with collectors. They have been re-issued periodically. Price varies with the date of production. Wonderful, whimsical forms. 4" long. Sevellec Henriot Q., c.1945.

On the right, a child's mug by Mathurin Meheut, an artist of the Henriot faïencerie. On the left, an ashtray featuring a biniou player, also by Meheut. Mug is 3" tall and 3" diameter. Ashtray is 5" diameter. Both marked Henriot Q, c.1930.

Perhaps the most popular of all the figural pieces produced by the faïenceries of Quimper! Nicot, known for his figures of elderly Bretons, produced two sizes of "The Three Gossips" for the Henriot factory, one 15 1/2" tall and this one 5 3/4" tall, 6 1/8" long, Henriot Q, c.1930.

Jim Sevellec, a prolific artist at the Henriot faïencerie, produced many small figures and a variety of dinnerware patterns. 7" diameter, Henriot Q on the back, J.E.Sev. on the front, c.1925.

During the same period, 1920 to 1940, a yellow glaze was introduced. Popular in the United States, it was sold in leading department stores. Both the yellow ware and the traditional white glazed wares were often marked with the name of the store in addition to the factory mark. I recall, as a young girl, admiring the yellow wares in R.H. Stearns of Boston. There are wares marked "Bloomingdales", "Ovington" and "Altman" from New York and "Carson Pirie Scott" and "Marshall Field" in Chicago, as well as numerous others. Macy's had their own mark, a star enclosed in a circle with the letters "MACY'S" in the circle.

Simple yellow ladle. 6" long. Henriot, c.1945.

Yellow glazed Quimper ware was introduced in the 1930s. Wonderful dragon handled teapot and sugar bowl, both with *fleur de lys* finials and a *sujet ordinaire*. Henriot Q, c.1935.

The form of this breakfast cup and saucer is delightful. The ever popular bagpipe! Yellow glaze, combined with blue ribbons, blue and red scallop and dot design, green foliage and a Bretonne combine in an altogether choice piece. Saucer is 6" long, Henriot Q, c.1935.

A tan glaze was also introduced at this time and most notable is the *Ivoire Corbeille* pattern mentioned earlier.

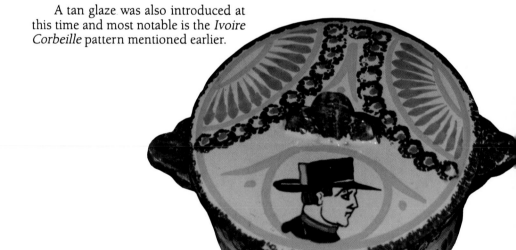

The tan glaze was introduced c. 1925 and this *bonbonière*, decorated in the *Ivoire Corbeille* pattern, is the most popular pattern of the tan glazed wares. 5" diameter, HB Q, c. 1925.

- Unmarked wares

These early, unmarked wares are typical examples of wares produced in the last half of the 19th century. Not only do the patterns indicate age but, more importantly, the characteristics of the clay, the glaze and the painting are indicative of 19th century production.

An early, unsigned, sponge decorated jug. Cobalt blue sponging was very popular in the 18th and 19th centuries and is produced in the faiencerie today. This fine example has a thick pedestal base and thin, black stripes that are typical of early wares. Yellow bands and touches of orange, blue and green complete the décor. A fine, early piece in superb condition. 7" tall, unmarked, c.1860.

Spongeware mug with yellow and black bands. This mug has all the earmarks of an early piece–the black bands, thick base, glaze irregularities and paint smudges. 4" tall, unmarked, c.1875.

A wonderfully shaped mug for beer. Same qualities as the previous two pieces. 4 1/2" tall, unmarked, c.1860.

Porringers were used as bowls and plates in the 18th century and still today! This example dates from the late 18th century. 3" tall, 8" across, unmarked, c.1880.

Plates decorated in geometric patterns enjoy great popularity today, as they surely did when this plate was produced. 8 1/2" diameter, unsigned, c.1860.

A superb example of an early geometric pattern. Yellow, blue and black bands ring a center medallion of *croisille décor* and a wonderful pattern of blue stripes and orange and green touches. 8 1/2" diameter, unmarked, c.1880.

-Comparing wares

Grande Maison and Henriot products

Because both the Grande Maison and the Henriot factories produced very similar wares at various times, these photos will afford you the opportunity to compare and identify the origin of some of these wares.

Opposite top:

The Grande Maison produced a series of plates with this delicately drawn border décor, featuring a man or woman in the naive yet detailed style. Scalloped rim, pinkish tinge. 9 1/2" diameter, HBQ, c.1910.

Pair of plates from the Henriot faïencerie, very similar to the Grande Maison plate on the next page. The figures are much less detailed but, in every other aspect, the plates are very similar! 9 1/2" diameter, HR, c. 1900.

Opposite bottom:

Three plates with *gros filets* or concentric yellow and blue bands, each from a different time period and factory, therefore, each a different price. Left. 8" diameter, Henriot Q, c.1930. Right. 7" diameter, HRQ, c.1925. Foreground. 7" diameter, HBQ, c.1940.

Miniature bellows to hold matches or little
blossoms hangs on the wall. *Croisillé* sides
and handle, very soft colors. HRQ, c.1910.
Compare this example with the bellows in
the next photo.

The Grande Maison produced this bellows
in the 1950s. Colors are sharp. This piece
lacks the slight irregularities seen in earlier
wares. A wonderful form, regardless of age.
4 3/4" tall, HBQ, c.1950.

-Similar wares

There are two faïenceries whose wares are often mistaken for the wares of Quimper. The most famous, or infamous, imitator of Quimper ware was a faïencerie near Le Mans, in the town of Malicorne. Near the end of the nineteenth century, Leon Pouplard, a potter from Malicorne, traveled to Brittany. He returned to Malicorne with the image of the *Petit Breton* in his mind and promptly decorated his wares in the same style. Further, Monsieur Pouplard adopted as his mark, his initial "P" combined with that of his wife Béatrix "B". When first used, the "P" was backwards. Later the "P" was turned and in 1898 the Porquier faïencerie filed suit charging that the "PB" of Malicorne too closely resembled the Porquier "PB". The court ruled against Pouplard and he was ordered to add an "x", as a footnote to his "PB" mark.

Malicone wares imitated those of Quimper and this pair of tall tumblers, with a magnificent *fleur de lys* on each, certainly isvery similar to the HB *lys* pattern. 4 1/4" tall, PBx (Malicorne), c.1900.

Banette or tray with a magnificent scene in a peasant's cottage! The colors are superb. The beautifully scalloped rim is trimmed in gold. *Décor riche b*order done in two lovely shades of blue. This is a Malicorne piece but obviously was inspired by Alfred Beau's designs for the Porquier faiencerie. 16" long, 10" wide, unsigned, c.1900.

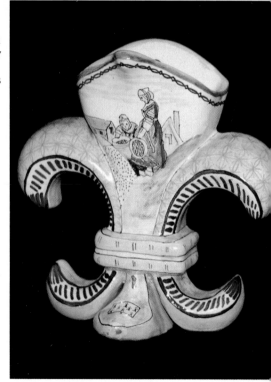

Trefoil shaped vase from Malicorne is decorated with a lovely scene of mother and child. The form was certainly borrowed from Quimper ware. 6 1/2" tall, early PB mark (the P is backwards), c.1880.

Octagonal plate with a bright yellow and blue *décor riche* scalloped border features a scene lifted from a Porquier plate. They are identical! 8" diameter, unmarked, Malicorne, c. 1890.

Large Malicorne charger with a lovely scene that is exactly the same as the scene on the "PB" plate titled "Roscoff" shown on page 39. Compare them! 12" diameter, unsigned, c. 1890.

Desvres, in northern France, has been a pottery making center for 200 years. The wares produced in Desvres were varied, including scenes and patterns easily confused with the wares of Quimper. A variety of marks were used by the factories in Desvres.

A 12" tall vase from the Desvres factory. This is obviously meant to capitalize on the great popularity of the faïence of Quimper. unmarked, c.1915.

-Wares for dolls

Delightful little tea sets for tea parties with dolls or teddy bears were produced. This *petit service de thé*, in a yellow glaze, is a complete set! Whimsical geometric patterns adorn dolls' plates which were produced in a variety of sizes and shapes. Doll's cups and mugs, pitchers and bowls are sweet.

Petit service de thé , for your dolls in a yellow glaze, is a complete set!
Tray is 10" long, tea pot is 2" tall, Henriot Q., c.1935.

Geometric patterns were often used on doll's dishes and these two, with scalloped rims, are great! 3" diameter, Henriot Q, c.1940.

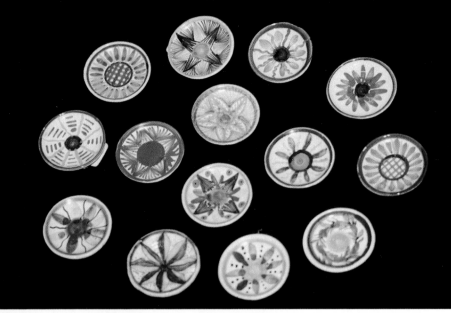

Dishes for your dolls. A different one for each doll! 2" diameter, all Henriot, c.1935.

The choice of patterns and shapes is endless! Four little dishes, 2" square with cut corners. Henriot Q, c.1930.

Little cups or mugs for dolls. A pair, one on either end, with blue and orange flowers. The other two, one with bleuets and one with flowers of blue dots. All 1 1/2" tall, all unmarked, the pair c.1935 and the other two, c.1920.

-Religious figures

Figures of Saints and holy water fonts have always enjoyed great popularity in France and were among the earliest of the wares produced in Quimper. Eighteenth century examples are displayed in Quimper's museums. Nineteenth and twentieth century examples are in great demand in France, a country with strong religious roots.

Holy water font with bright yellows and blues. Signed HRQ on the front, the *fleurs de lys* on the cup are lovely. 8" tall, c.1915.

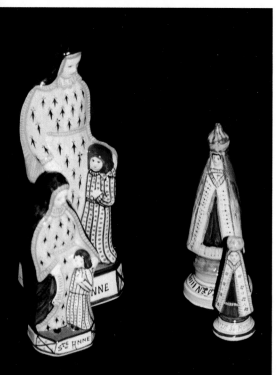

Religious statues of the Virgin and saints have always been very popular.

A sampling of religious statues produced in Quimper's faïenceries.

Chapter 4
SUMMARY

- Tips for Collectors

Throughout their three hundred year history, the faïenceries of Quimper have alternately struggled through difficult economic periods and thrived during periods of economic expansion. Their success can be directly attributed to the continuing production of classic wares such as the double handled porringer, while always exploring new techniques and introducing new forms, designs or glazes. As discussed in Chapter 2, when financial difficulties beset the Porquier faïencerie early in the twentieth century, the Henriot faïencerie purchased their patterns and molds. In 1968, the two remaining faïenceries merged. The modern, thriving faïencerie in Quimper today is a composite of the Grande Maison and the Porquier and Henriot faïenceries. The wares produced today represent some of the best designs of years past as well as new patterns and molds created especially for today's market.

Today, wares are still painted entirely by hand in a modern facility owned by Americans Paul and Sarah Janssens. The faïencierie employs about one hundred people and is a popular stop on the itinerary of many visitors to Brittany. A tour of the factory should be followed by a visit to the Musée de la Faïence Jules Verlingue which is located just behind the factory. The display of wares in the museum is complete and breathtaking, from the fragments of early eighteenth century wares to the life size figure of a young Bretonne maiden, from early sponged porringers to an exquisite platter decorated by Alfred Beau with a Breton scene.

In 1990, the Musée des Beaux Arts de Quimper mounted an exhibit spanning three-hundred years of production in Quimper's faïenceries. For those who did not see the exhibit, the museum catalog will take you there, from pre-historic and Gallo-Roman times to contemporary production. Especially noteworthy were the African busts sculpted by Emile Monier in 1931 and the musical instruments, a violin (HB) by Paul Hagemans and a clarinet and clarion (PB) in the Rouen décor. In addition to a marvelous collection of faïence, the museum's collection of Breton paintings, especially those of Jean-Julian Lemordant, is magnificent. The Musée Departmental Breton also deserves a visit. Their wonderful collection of faïence is complemented with a fascinating display of traditional Breton costumes and furniture.

Collecting Quimper is an individual pursuit because of the myriad of wares to choose from. Typically, a collector's first few purchases are impulsive, items that attract their eye and captivate their spirit. After a while, many collectors focus on one pattern, a particular form, a certain period, glaze color or mark, while always searching for the perfect piece. The quest can be exciting, at times frustrating, and always informative.

When establishing the value of a piece of Quimper ware, first research the mark and then consider the age, condition, rarity and excellence of design. To establish the age of a piece of Quimper ware, several qualities should be noted. First, carefully observe the effects of the molding process. Early handmade wares and early, primitive molds were often uneven, resulting in irregular forms while modern casting methods employed after World War II produced evenly shaped wares. Have you noticed the occasional plate with a dip in the rim? Second, carefully observe the qualities of the glaze. Early wood fired kilns often resulted in a runny, uneven glaze while modern electric ovens, also introduced after World War II, insure a smoother glaze with a high sheen. Third, examine the underside of each piece. Often, there are three small lines in the glaze on the underside of a piece. These lines indicate that the piece was placed on a tripod during firing, a practice discontinued soon after World War II. Irregularities are always more easily observed on the underside of most pieces. In general, bolder colors were introduced between the two World Wars.

Condition is another serious consideration when determining the value of a piece of Quimper. While pristine condition is considered most desirable, it is not mandatory. An important example of Quimper ware is only slightly impaired if it has minor damage. Consider a platter decorated by Alfred Beau with a detailed scene of a Breton celebration. The presence of a small old flake, chip or age line has little or no effect on price. The same is true for a hard-to-find piece such as a candlestick or snuff. Any restoration work should be done by a professional because poor restoration work can be more compromising than a small, honest chip. Large chips or cracks certainly do compromise the integrity of any piece.

Rarity and quality of design greatly effect the price. Alfred Beau's designs for the Porquier faïencerie are both rare and considered masterpieces; thus, they command very high prices, as much as five to ten thousand dollars. Snuffs in unusual forms, figural candlesticks, jardinières, figures of saints, inkwells and many more items distinctively designed and/or produced in limited quantities also command healthy prices.

At every opportunity, examine the wares carefully. Train your eye and your mind. Visit antiques shops and attend shows as often as possible. Ask questions of the person exhibiting Quimper ware, and read. The Bibliography accompanying this text lists the best books available on old Quimper ware.

Libbey Glass was licensed to use the Petit Breton on beverage glasses.

150 ❖

Bibliography

Bondhus, Sandra V., *Quimper Pottery: A French Folk Art Faïence,* 1981.

Datesman, Joan, *Collecting Quimper, Quimper Collections.*

Mali, Millicent S., *French Faïence: Fantasie et Populaire of the 19th and 20th Centuries,* United Printing, 1986.

Musée des Beaux-Arts, *Quimper Trois Siècles de Faïences 1690 - 1990 Catalogue,* Editions Ouèst-France Ville de Quimper, 1990.

Quimper Trois Siècles de Faïences 1690 - 1990. Editions Ouèst-France Ville de Quimper, 1990.

Roullot, Michel J., *Les Faïences Artistiques de Quimper aux XVIII et XIX Siècles,* Lorient, Art-Média, 1980.

Taburet, Marjatta, *La Faïence de Quimper,* Paris, Editions Sous le Vent, 1979.

Taburet, Marjatta, *Quimper Faïence,* Editions Ouest-France-Ville de Quimper, 1984.

Verlingue, Bernard Jules and Mannoni, Edith, *Les Faïences de Quimper,* Paris, Massin Editeur.

Price Guide

This listing is intended to be used only as a general guide. Values vary immensely according to the condition of the piece, the location of the market, and the overall quality of design and manufacture. Prices vary between regions, and between specialty shops and general shows.

The left hand column of this guide shows the page number on which you can find each item. The center column indicates the position of the item on that page (T=top, B=bottom, C=center, R=right, L=left). The right hand column provides an estimated value. The prices in this guide reflect pieces in mint or near mint condition.

page	position	price range	page	position	price range
10	TR	950	23	T	220 each
	B	600/pair		B	220
11	R	95	24	TR	125
12	T	65		B	800
	B	125	25	T	475
13	T	325		B	450
	B	150	26	T	475
14	TR	195		B	160
	B	475	27	T	450
15	L	650		B	145, 175
	R	675	28	B	625
16	T	450	29	T	85
	B	225		B	225
17	T	90/pair	30	T	125/pair
	B	450		B	140, 100
18	CL	300	31	L	195
	TR	95		TR	175
	BR	175		BR	175
19	TR	175	32	BL	180
	B	175		TR	190
20	T	125	33	T	525
	B	225		B	650
21	BL	160	34	TL	120
	TR	160		TR	275
22	TL	60		B	160
	B	125	35	T	275
	TR	140		B	45 each

36	T	250			BR	140
	B	950		65	TL	295
37		140			BL	575
38	T	1200		66	T	700/pair
	B	1200			B	495
39	T	1100		67	TL	125
	B	1100			CR	75
40		1600			B	60
42	T	950		68	TL	185
	B	175			TR	275
43		2500			B	75
44	T	195		69	T	175
	B	800			B	225
45	T	220		70	TL	1000
	B	195			BR	195
46	T	900		71	T	750
	B	225			BL	325
47	TR	275		72		950
	BR	375		74	T	165
48		225			BL	140
49	T	450			BR	165
	B	550		75	T	175
50	TL	325			B	175
	B	750		76	T	160
51	T	450			B	110
	B	650		77	T	195
52	T	325			B	240
	B	450		78	T	525
53	T	350			B	525
	B	350		79	T	375
54	T	110			B	325
	B	100/pair		80	T	525
55	TL	750/pair			B	325
	BL	225		81	T	250
	R	220			B	250
56		900/pair		82		550
57	T	110/pair		83	TL	495
	B	325			R	350
58	T	575		84	T	110
	B	150			B	95 each
59	TL	90		85	T	110, 90
	BL	675			BL	120
	TR	160			BR	160
60	T	900		86	T	60, 60, 30, 75
	BR	140			B	85
61	L	450		87	T	65, 80
	R	550			B	425
62	T	160		88	TL	325
	B	425			B	275
63	T	475		89	T	275
	B	350			B	175
64	TL	165		90	T	225

No.	Code	Value
	B	225
91	T	225
	B	650
92	T	350
	B	150
93	T	350
	B	450 each
94		190
95	L	230
	R	225
96	T	175
	B	175
97	T	150
	B	275
98	T	220
	B	350
99	T	375
	B	350
100	T	450
	B	475
101	T	375
	B	325
102	T	175, 175, 150
	B	325
103	T	60 each
	BL	175
	BR	150
104	T	325 each
	CL	325
	BR	240
105	T	150
	B	295
106	T	1100
	BL	65
	BR	195
107	T	150, 195, 150
	B	120
115		650
116	T	195
	B	175
117	BL	145
	TR	145
	BR	175
118	T	325
	B	125
119		55, 85
120	T	425
	B	225
121	T	225
	B	150
122	T	325
	B	65 each
123	T	350
	B	325
124	T	250
	B	150
125	T	60
	B	195
126	T	275
	B	75
127	T	450
	B	250
128	T	195
	B	155
129	T	275
	B	450
130	T	450
	B	275
131	T	120
	B	65, 95
132	T	350
	B	160
133	T	95
	B	375
134	T	160
	B	175
135	T	260
	B	140
136	T	140
	B	80
137	T	175
	B	175
138		600/pair
139	T	450
	B	65, 65, 85
140	L	185
	R	125
141		85 each
142	T	900
	B	500
143	T	350
	B	550
144		275
145	T	195
	B	35 each
146	T	35 each
	CL	40 each
	B	45 each
147		340
148	T	175, 375
	B	175, 395
150		40 each
152		275
156		350 each

Two snuffs, both unsigned, 2" wide, 3" tall, c.
1900. Left: rare pansy décor on the front and
croisillé on the back. Right: Breton peasant
and *fleur de lys* on back.

Index